ALIEN INVASION: SPORTS EDITION

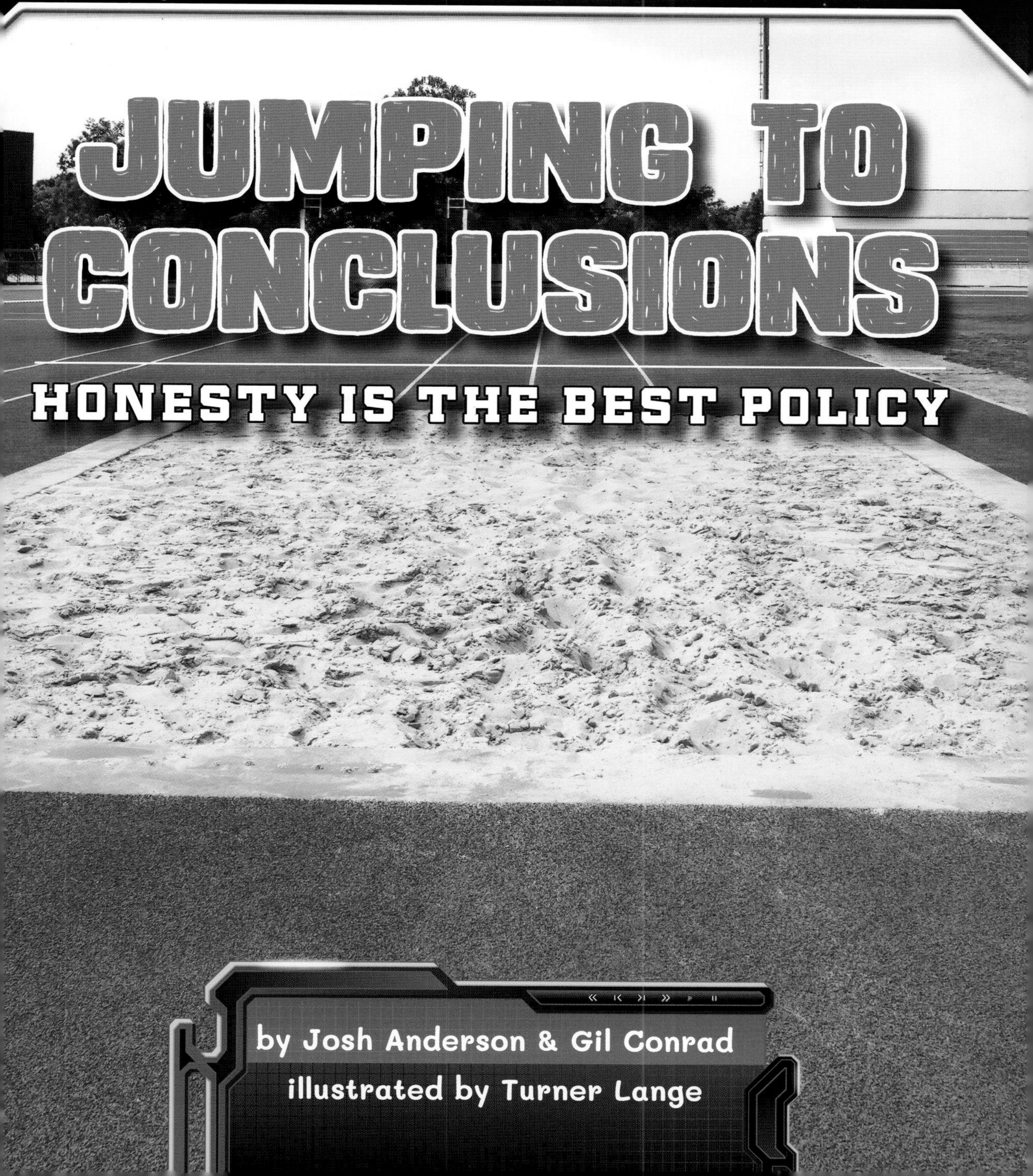

JUMPING TO CONCLUSIONS

HONESTY IS THE BEST POLICY

by Josh Anderson & Gil Conrad

illustrated by Turner Lange

TORCH GRAPHIC PRESS

Published in the United States of America by Cherry Lake Publishing Group
Ann Arbor, Michigan
www.cherrylakepublishing.com

Reading Adviser: Beth Walker Gambro, MS, Ed., Reading Consultant, Yorkville, IL

Book Design: Book Buddy Media

Photo Credits: page 1: ©DigitalVision Vectors / Getty Images; page 7: ©Carole Raddato / Wikimedia; page 13: ©Tony Duffy / Getty Images; page 27: ©Tetra images RF / Getty Images; clipboard background: ©t_kimura / Getty Images; galaxy background: ©vi73777 / Getty Images; track background: ©Soonthorn Wongsaita / Shutterstock

Torch Graphic Press is an imprint of Cherry Lake Publishing Group.

Library of Congress Cataloging-in-Publication Data has been filed and is available at catalog.loc.gov

Cherry Lake Publishing Group would like to acknowledge the work of the Partnership for 21st Century Learning, a Network of Battelle for Kids. Please visit http://www.battelleforkids.org/networks/p21 for more information.

Printed in the United States of America
Corporate Graphics

TABLE OF CONTENTS

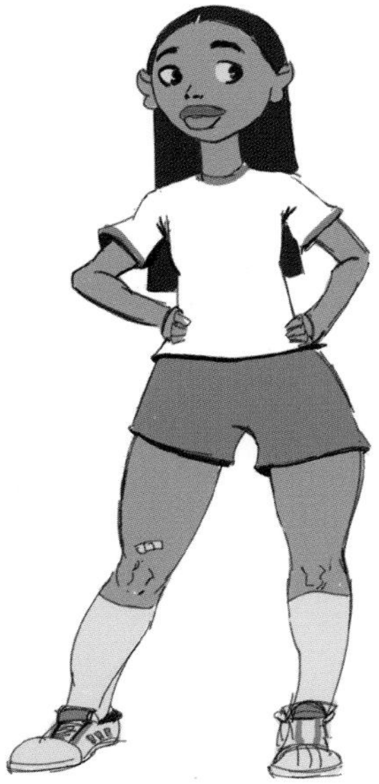

FRANCESCA DIAZ
FRANCESCA WORKS HARD AT THE LONG JUMP. BUT SHE'S ALWAYS COMING IN SECOND. WILL SHE EVER GET THE CHANCE TO WIN A MEDAL?

DREEPY
DREEPY IS AN INTERGALACTIC SPORTS STAR, AND SHE KNOWS IT. HER PLANET VALUES HONESTY OVER EVERYTHING. WHO WANTS TO GET SQUASHED BY A TRUTHY BOOT?

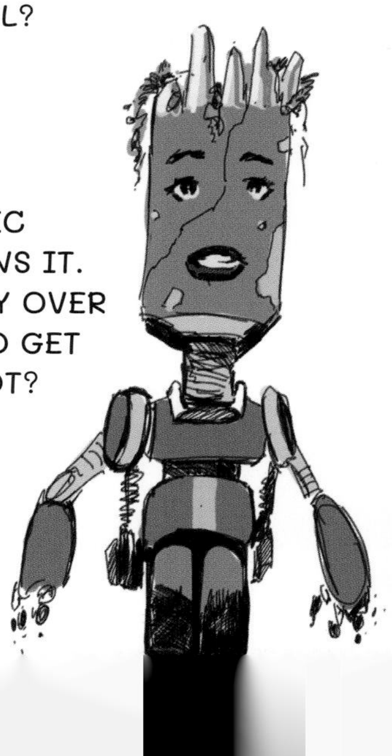

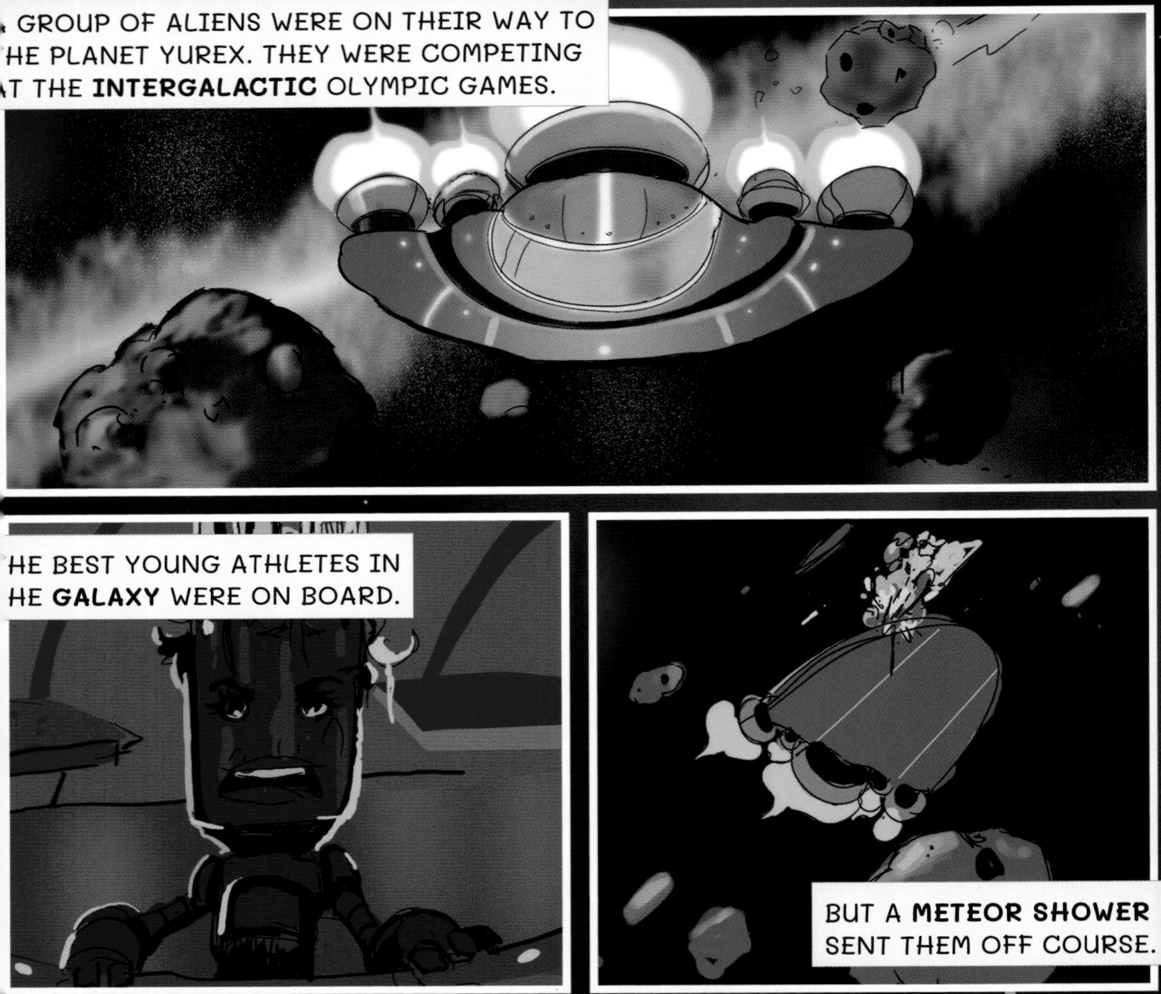

GROUP OF ALIENS WERE ON THEIR WAY TO
HE PLANET YUREX. THEY WERE COMPETING
T THE **INTERGALACTIC** OLYMPIC GAMES.
HE BEST YOUNG ATHLETES IN
HE **GALAXY** WERE ON BOARD.
BUT A **METEOR SHOWER**
SENT THEM OFF COURSE.

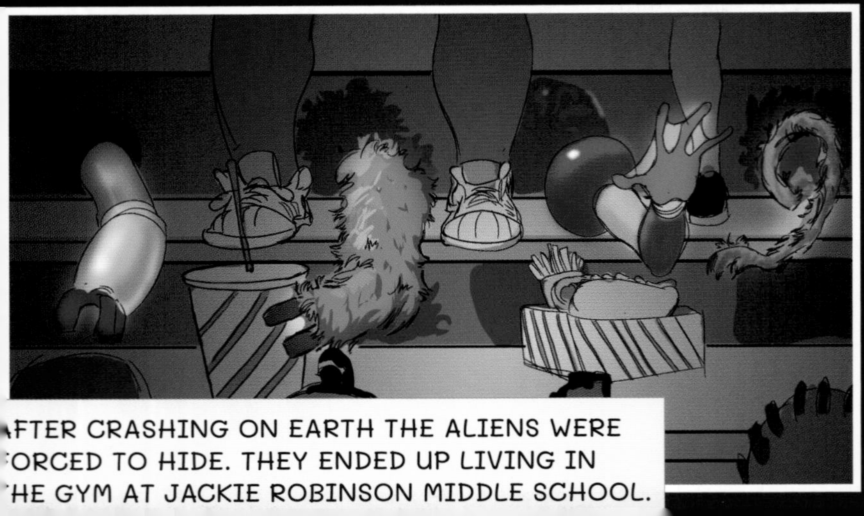

FTER CRASHING ON EARTH THE ALIENS WERE
ORCED TO HIDE. THEY ENDED UP LIVING IN
HE GYM AT JACKIE ROBINSON MIDDLE SCHOOL.

intergalactic: between galaxies in space

galaxy: a system of stars and their solar systems

meteor shower: a group of space rocks that fall as they enter Earth's atmosphere

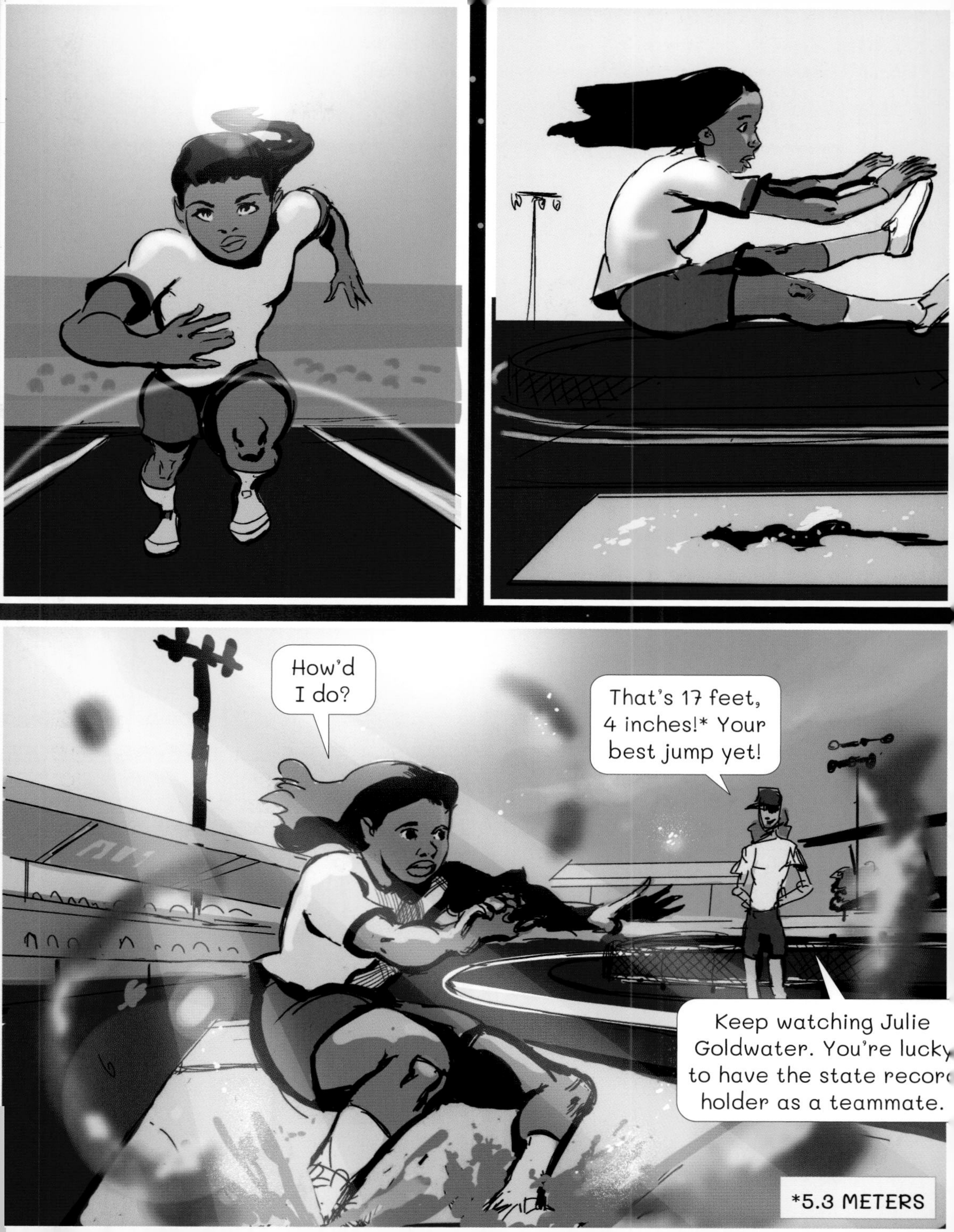
How'd I do?
That's 17 feet, 4 inches!* Your best jump yet!
Keep watching Julie Goldwater. You're lucky to have the state recor
holder as a teammate.
*5.3 METERS

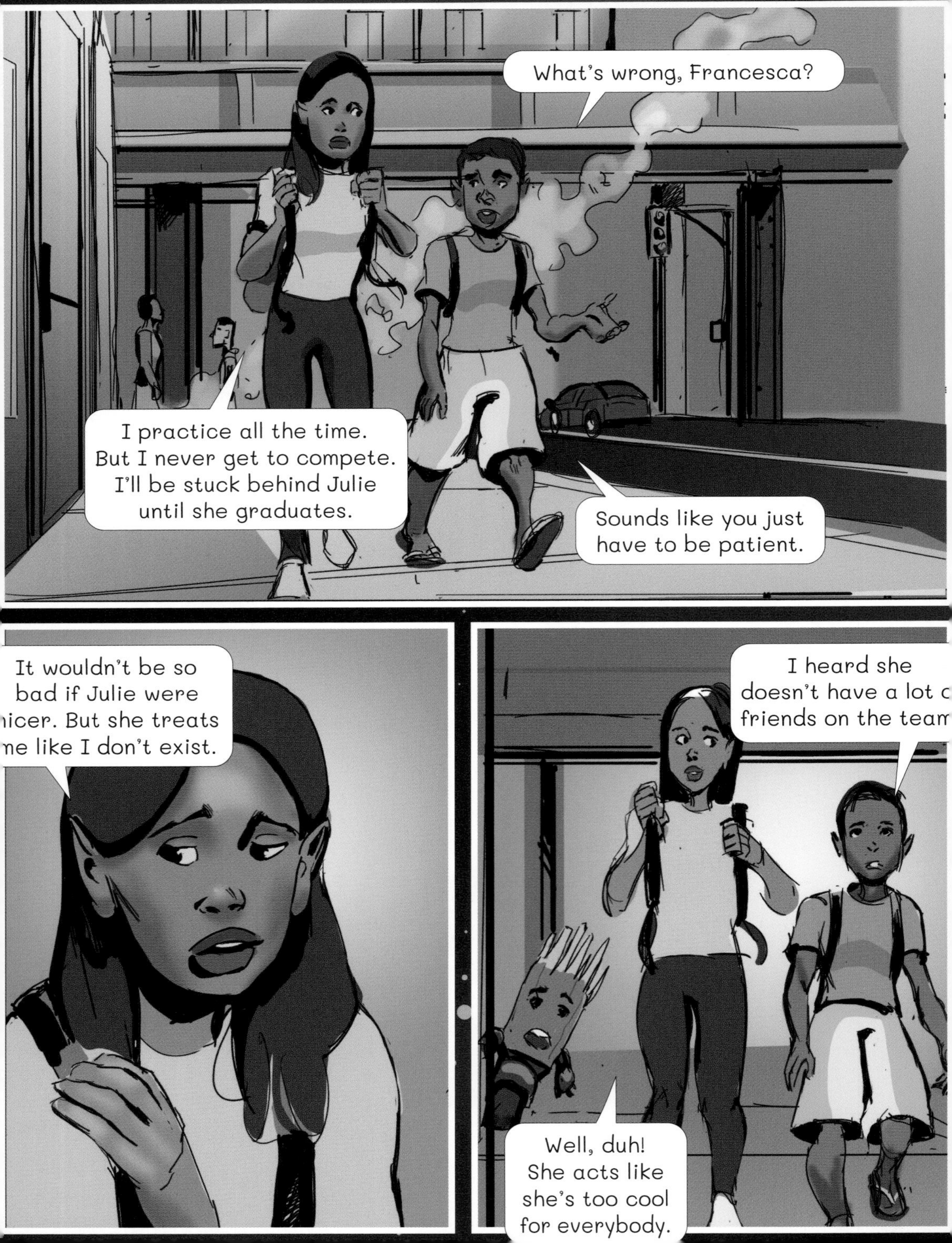
What's wrong, Francesca?
I practice all the time. But I never get to compete. I'll be stuck behind Julie until she graduates.
Sounds like you just have to be patient.
It wouldn't be so bad if Julie were icer. But she treats me like I don't exist.
I heard she doesn't have a lot friends on the team
Well, duh! She acts like she's too cool for everybody.

HISTORY OF THE LONG JUMP

The long jump has been around since ancient Greece. Their Olympians swung weights in their hands before jumping and then dropped them in mid-air. The jumpers believed this would help them create forward **momentum** to jump farther.

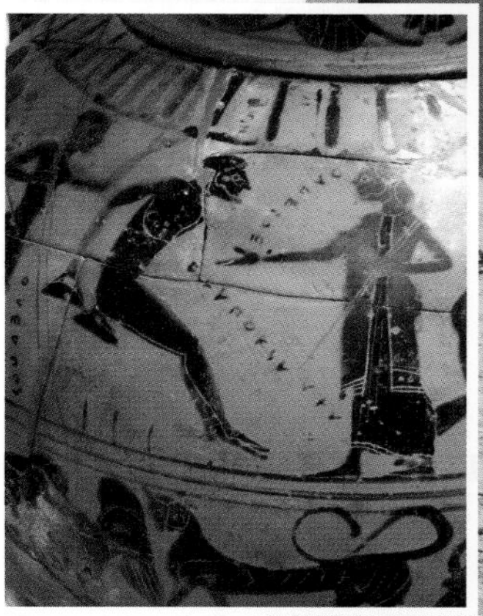

The long jump is broken into 4 parts: approach, takeoff, flight, and landing. Different skills are needed for each. For example, there are 3 different styles for flight. Athletes must experiment with the hang, the sail, and the hitch kick. Then, they decide which is best for them.

The long jump has been part of the modern Olympic Games since they were first held in 1896. The United States has won more gold medals in the long jump than all other countries combined.

momentum: the force or speed of motion an object has

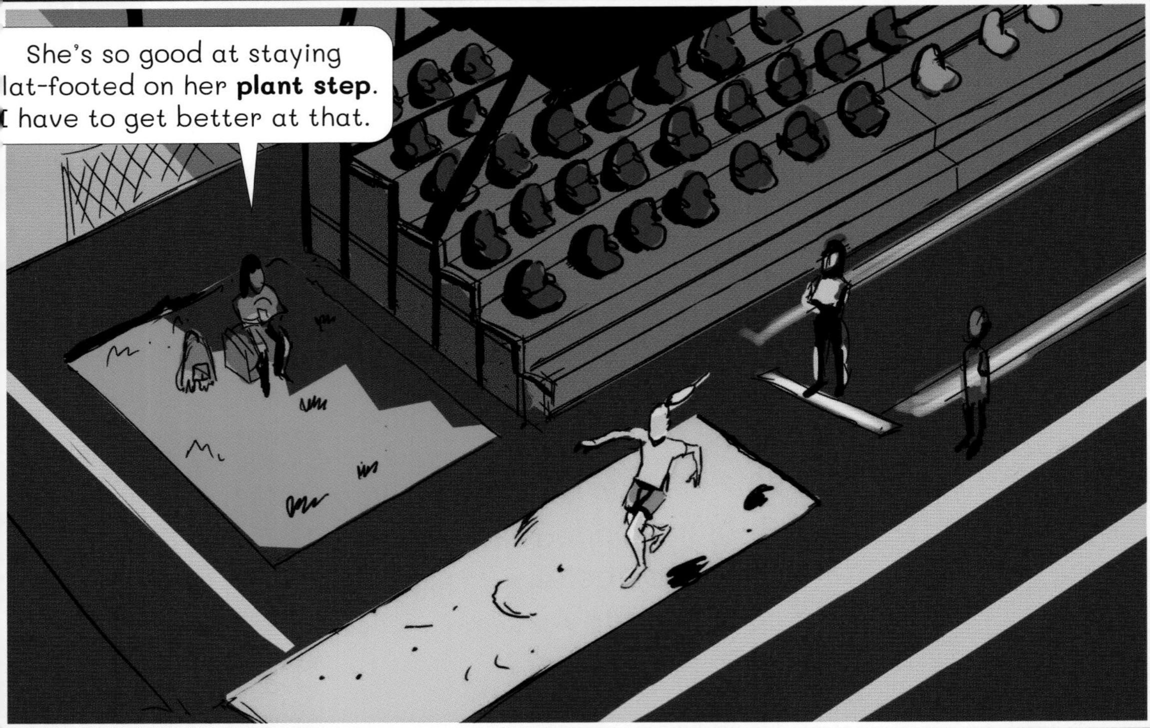
She's so good at staying lat-footed on her **plant step**. I have to get better at that.

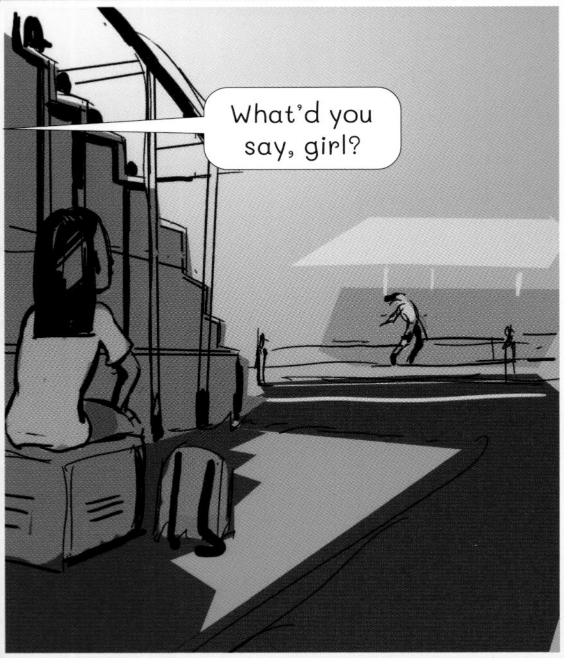
What'd you say, girl?

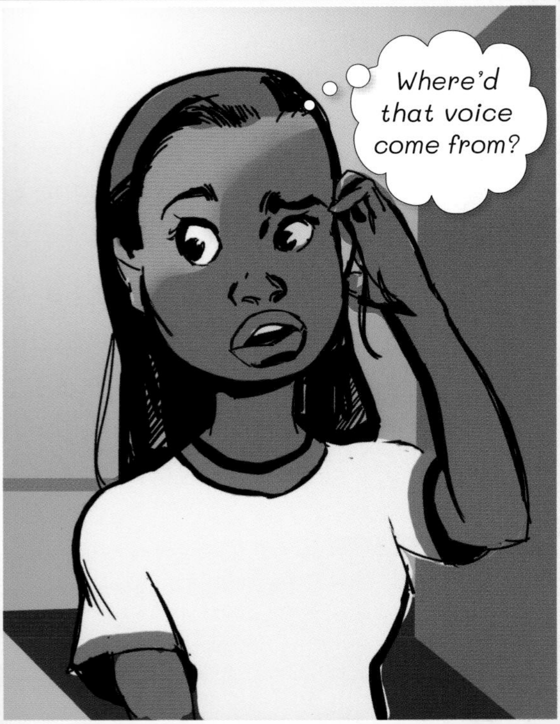
Where'd that voice come from?

plant step: the last step before a jump

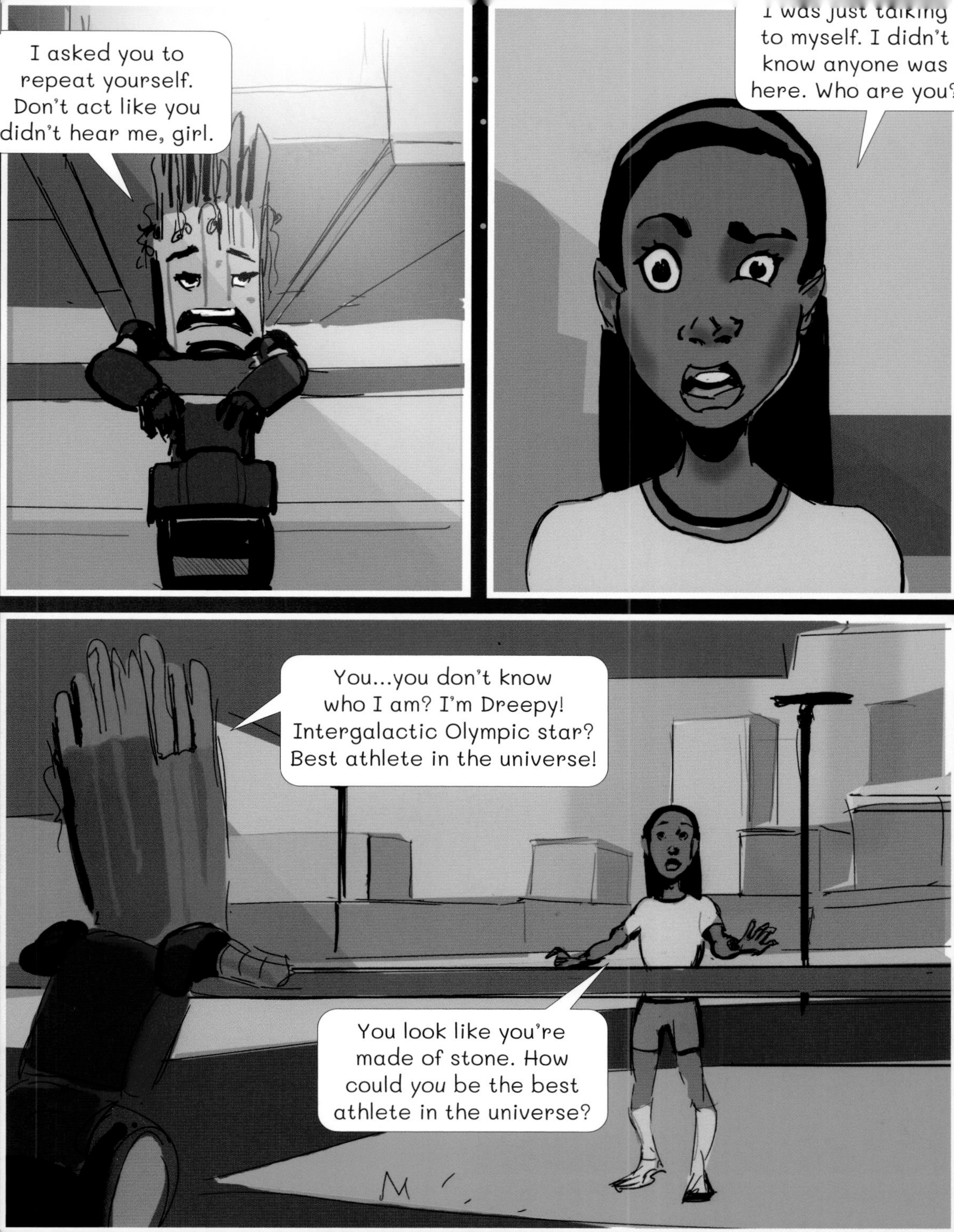
I asked you to repeat yourself. Don't act like you didn't hear me, girl.
I was just talking to myself. I didn't know anyone was here. Who are you?
You...you don't know who I am? I'm Dreepy! Intergalactic Olympic star? Best athlete in the universe!
You look like you're made of stone. How could *you* be the best athlete in the universe?

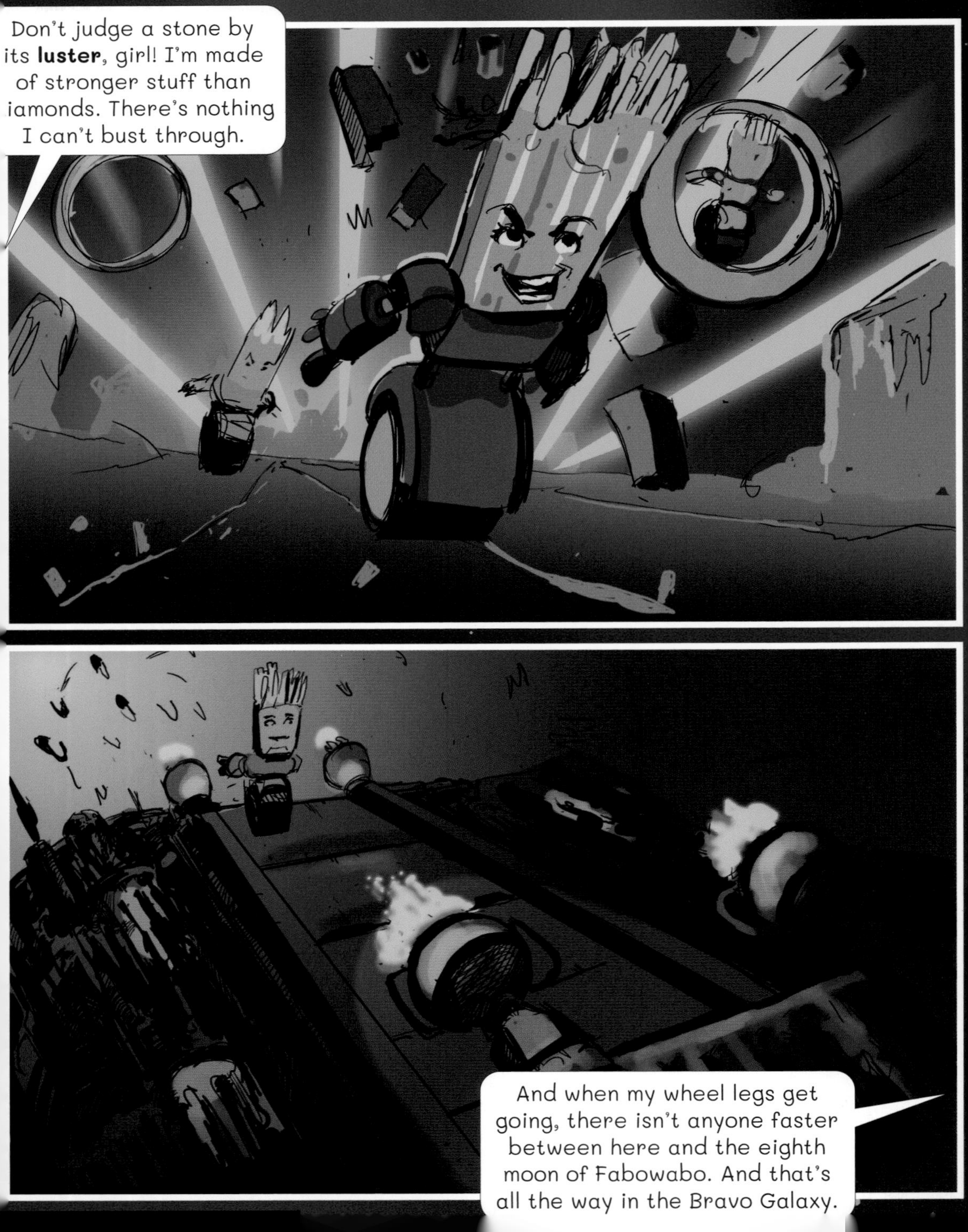
Don't judge a stone by its **luster**, girl! I'm made of stronger stuff than iamonds. There's nothing I can't bust through.
And when my wheel legs get going, there isn't anyone faster between here and the eighth moon of Fabowabo. And that's all the way in the Bravo Galaxy.

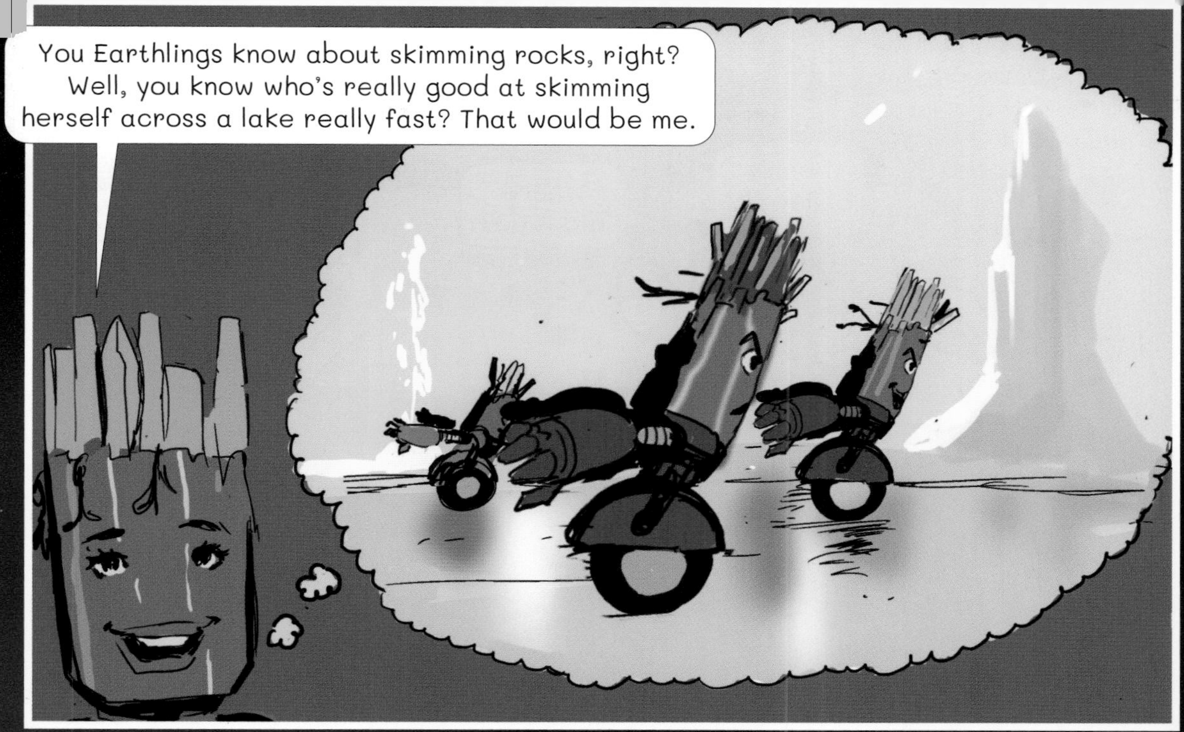
You Earthlings know about skimming rocks, right? Well, you know who's really good at skimming herself across a lake really fast? That would be me.

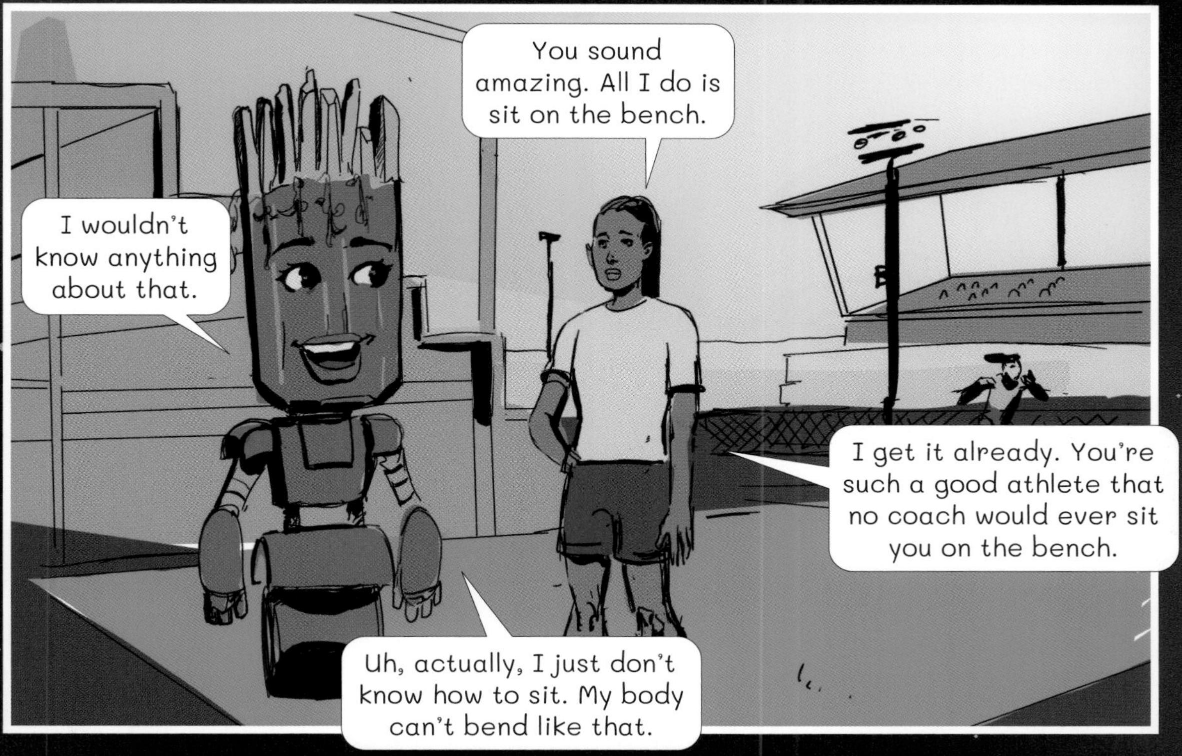
You sound amazing. All I do is sit on the bench.
I wouldn't know anything about that.
I get it already. You're such a good athlete that no coach would ever sit you on the bench.
Uh, actually, I just don't know how to sit. My body can't bend like that.

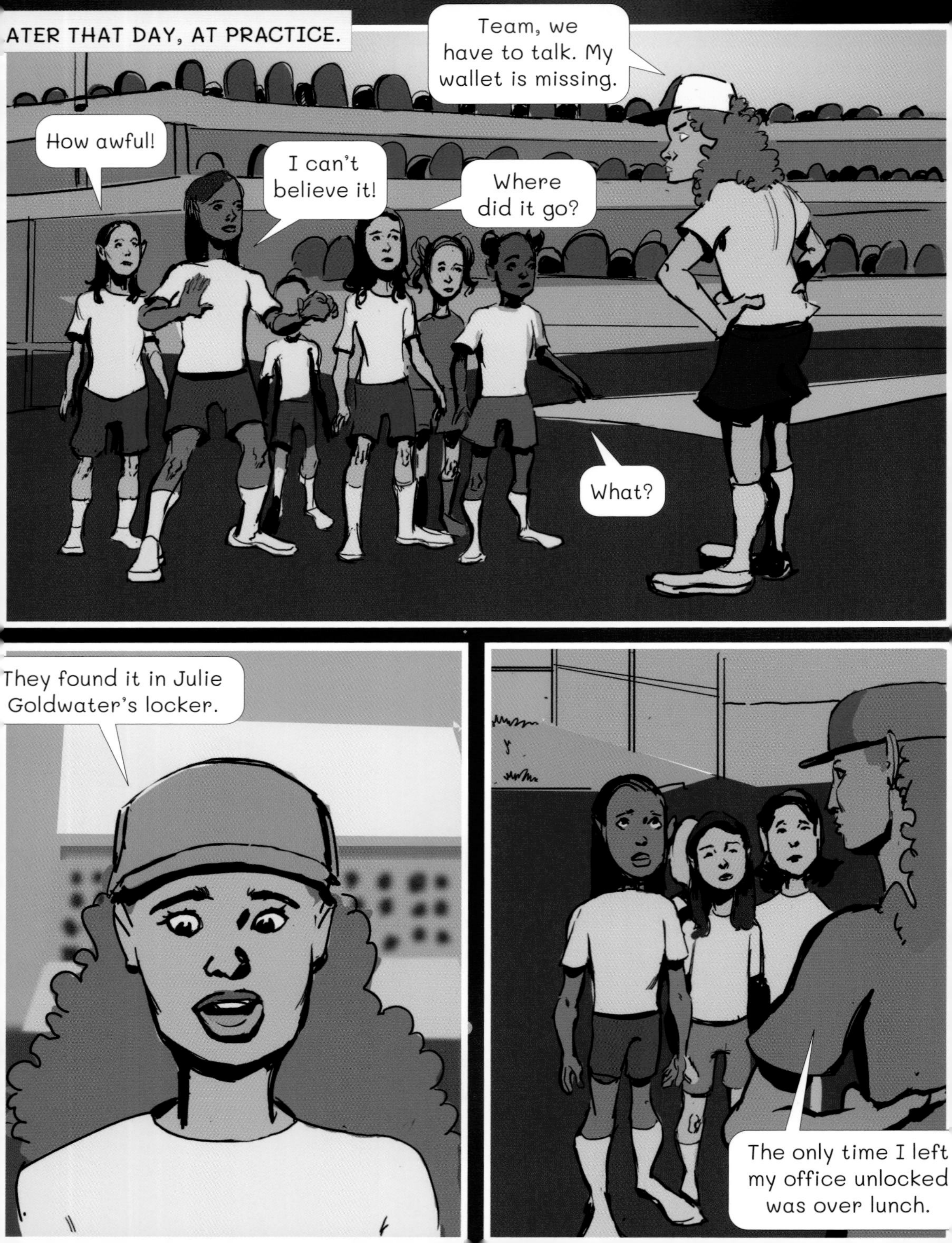
ATER THAT DAY, AT PRACTICE.
Team, we have to talk. My wallet is missing.
How awful!
I can't believe it!
Where did it go?
What?
They found it in Julie Goldwater's locker.
The only time I left my office unlocked was over lunch.

THE GOAT

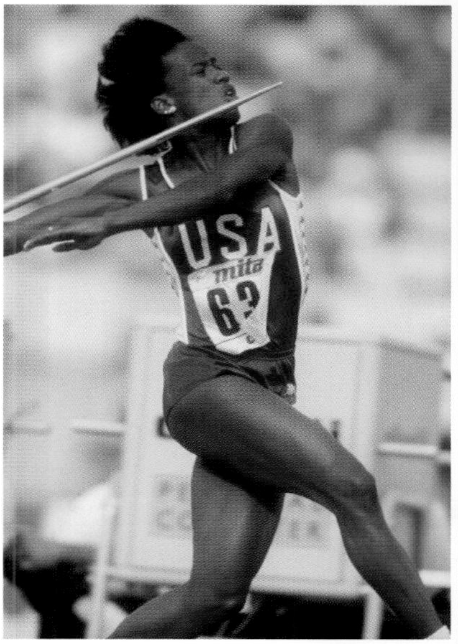
USA
mita

Jackie Joyner-Kersee is one of the greatest athletes of all time. Joyner-Kersee competed in 4 different Olympics from 1984 to 1996. She won medals at each of them. She also participated in the heptathlon. In the heptathlon, athletes compete in 7 different events, which test running, throwing, and jumping.

In high school, Joyner-Kersee nearly qualified for the Olympics. In college, she competed in both basketball and track and field.

Joyner-Kersee was diagnosed with **asthma** in college. With help from doctors, Joyner-Kersee was able to overcome the condition. Today, she speaks to people around the world. She wants everyone to be more successful in sports and in life.

asthma: a condition that makes breathing difficult

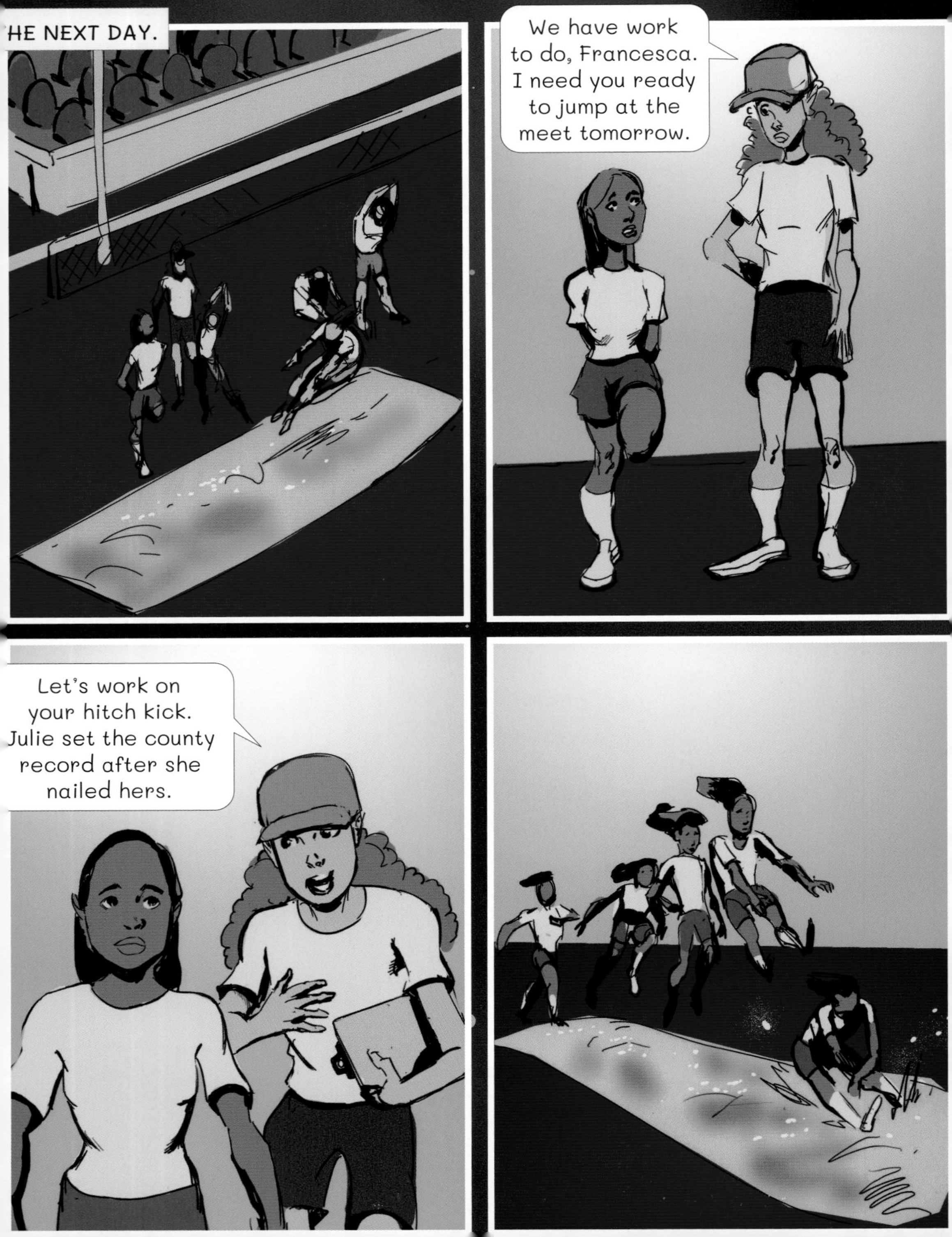
THE NEXT DAY.
We have work to do, Francesca. I need you ready to jump at the meet tomorrow.
Let's work on your hitch kick. Julie set the county record after she nailed hers.

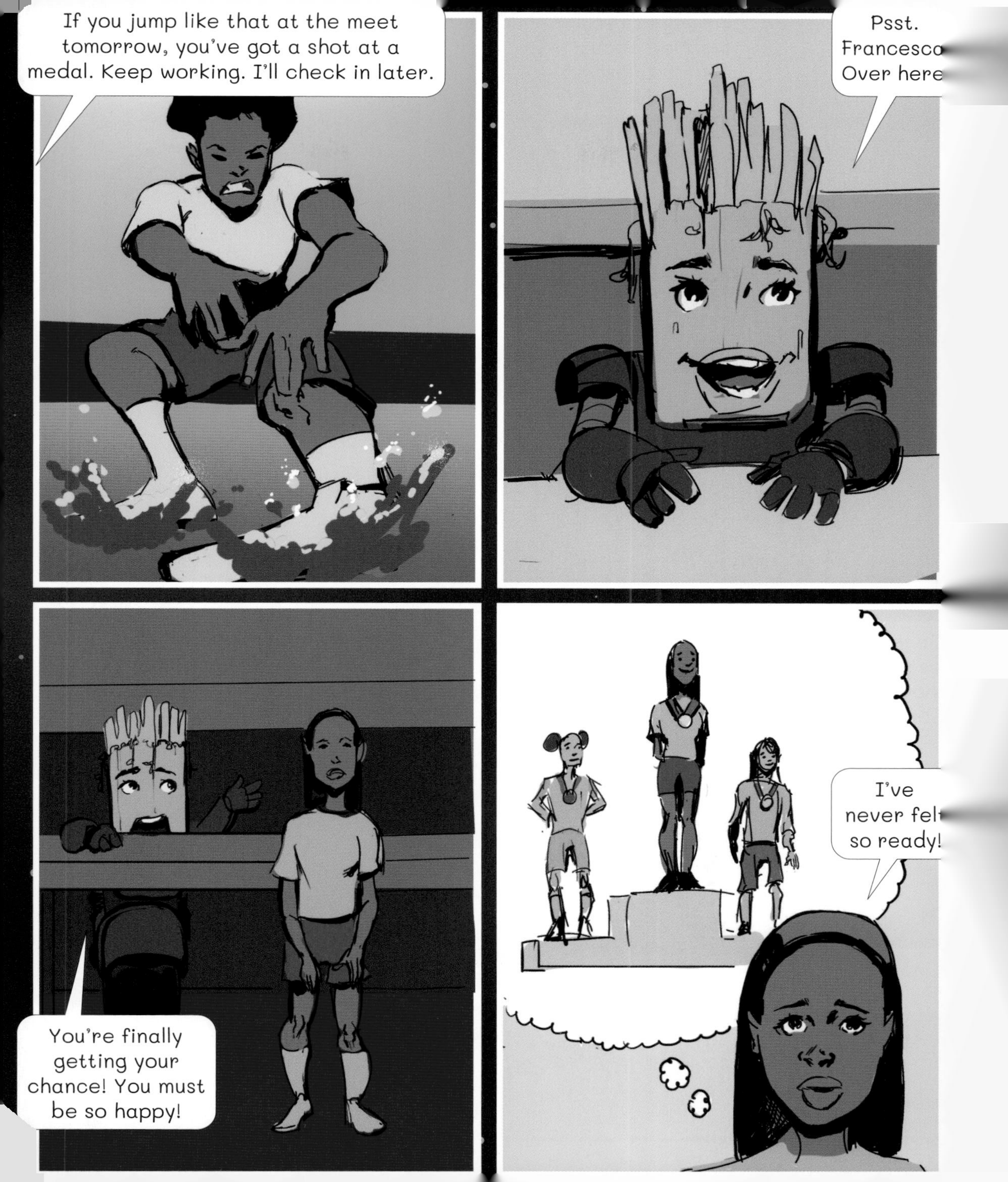
If you jump like that at the meet tomorrow, you've got a shot at a medal. Keep working. I'll check in later.
Psst. Francesca Over here
You're finally getting your chance! You must be so happy!
I've never felt so ready!

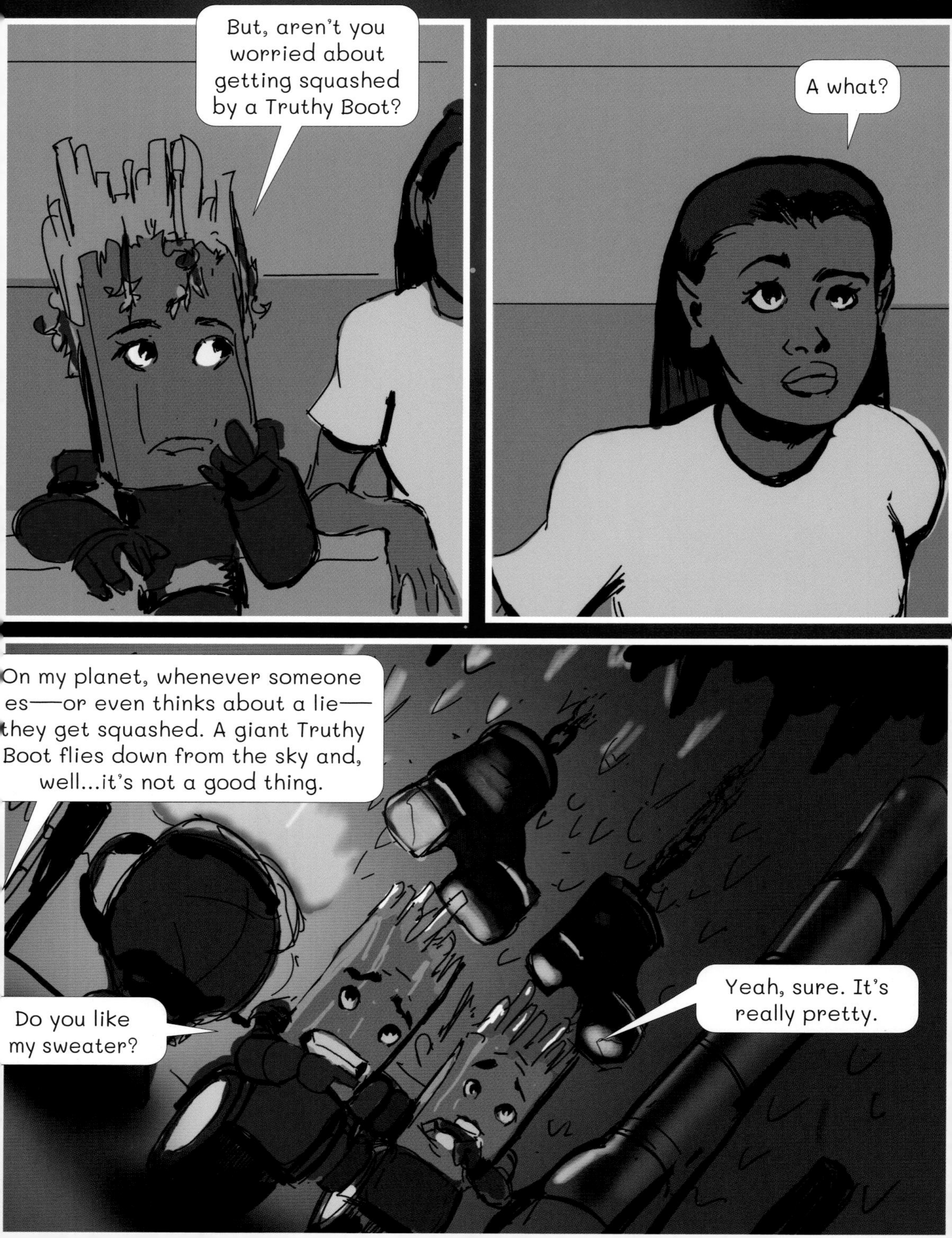
But, aren't you worried about getting squashed by a Truthy Boot?
A what?
On my planet, whenever someone es—or even thinks about a lie—they get squashed. A giant Truthy Boot flies down from the sky and, well...it's not a good thing.
Do you like my sweater?
Yeah, sure. It's really pretty.

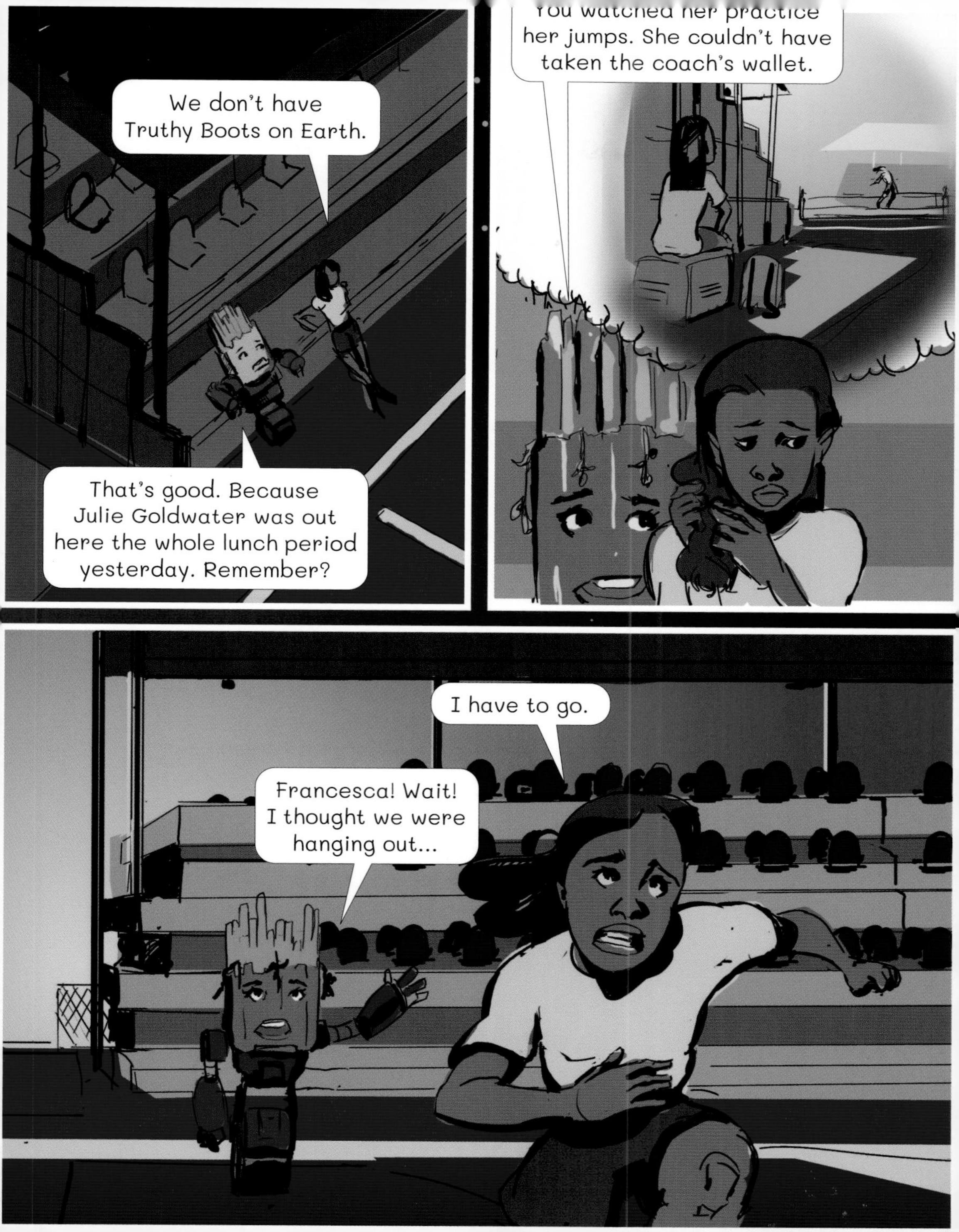
We don't have Truthy Boots on Earth.
That's good. Because Julie Goldwater was out here the whole lunch period yesterday. Remember?
You watched her practice her jumps. She couldn't have taken the coach's wallet.
I have to go.
Francesca! Wait! I thought we were hanging out...

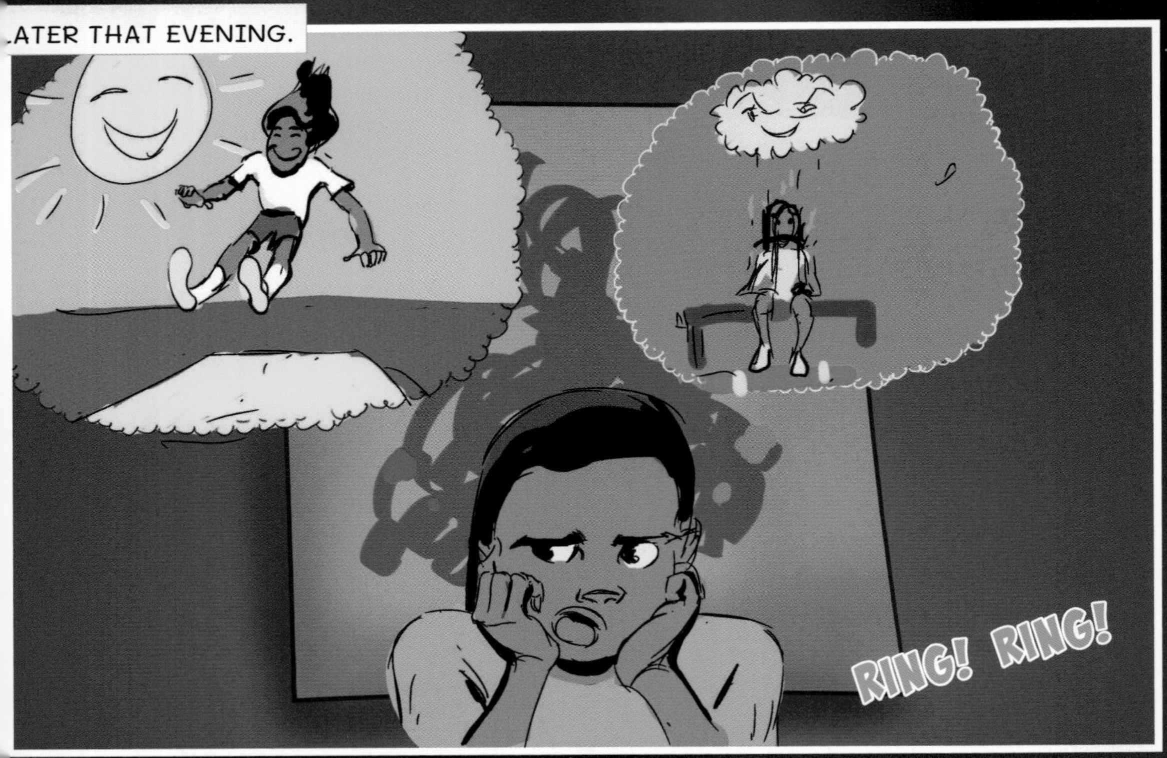
LATER THAT EVENING.
RING! RING!

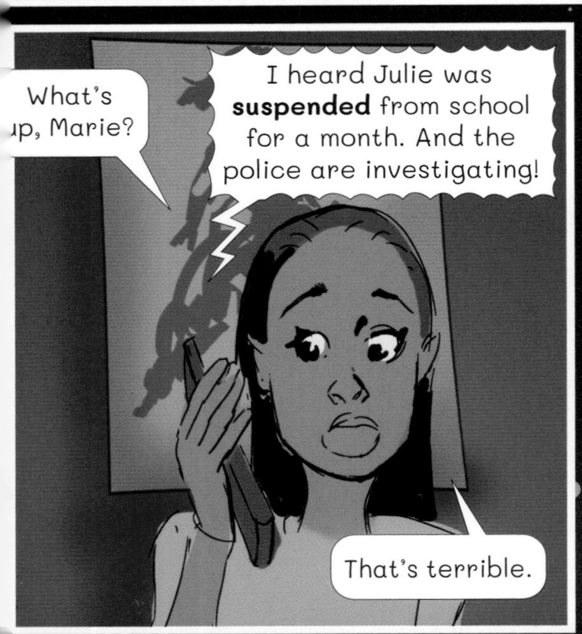
What's up, Marie?
I heard Julie was **suspended** from school for a month. And the police are investigating!
That's terrible.

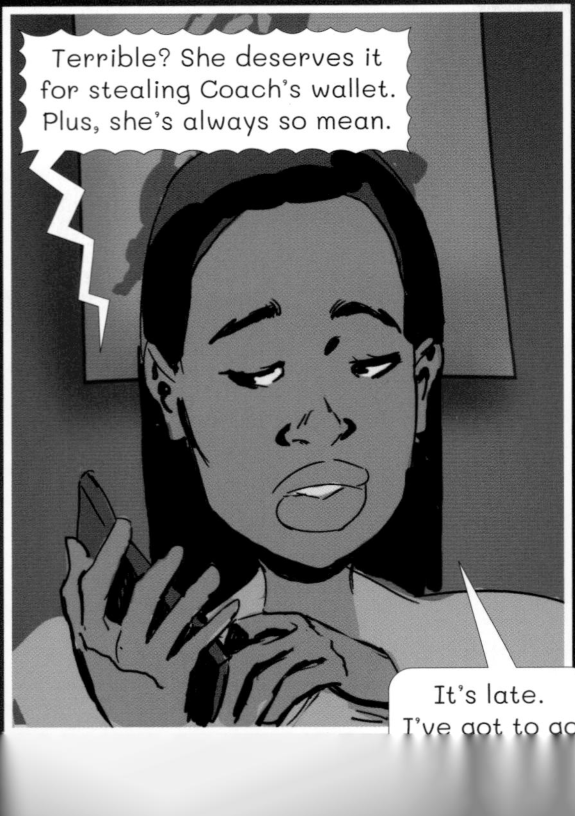
Terrible? She deserves it for stealing Coach's wallet. Plus, she's always so mean.
It's late. I've got to go

suspended: not allowed to attend school or be part of a program

THAT NIGHT, FRANCESCA BARELY SLEPT AT ALL.

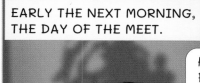

EARLY THE NEXT MORNING, THE DAY OF THE MEET.

Hi, Julie. It's Francesca... from the track team.

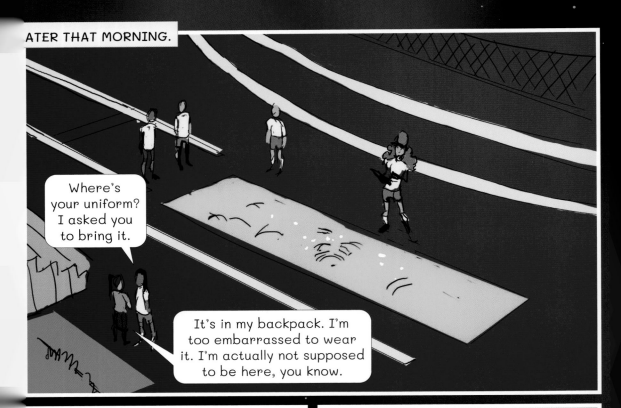

Where's your uniform? I asked you to bring it.

It's in my backpack. I'm too embarrassed to wear it. I'm actually not supposed to be here, you know.

Excuse me? Coach?

Goldwater, what are you doing here? I believe I was clear that you are off the team... permanently!

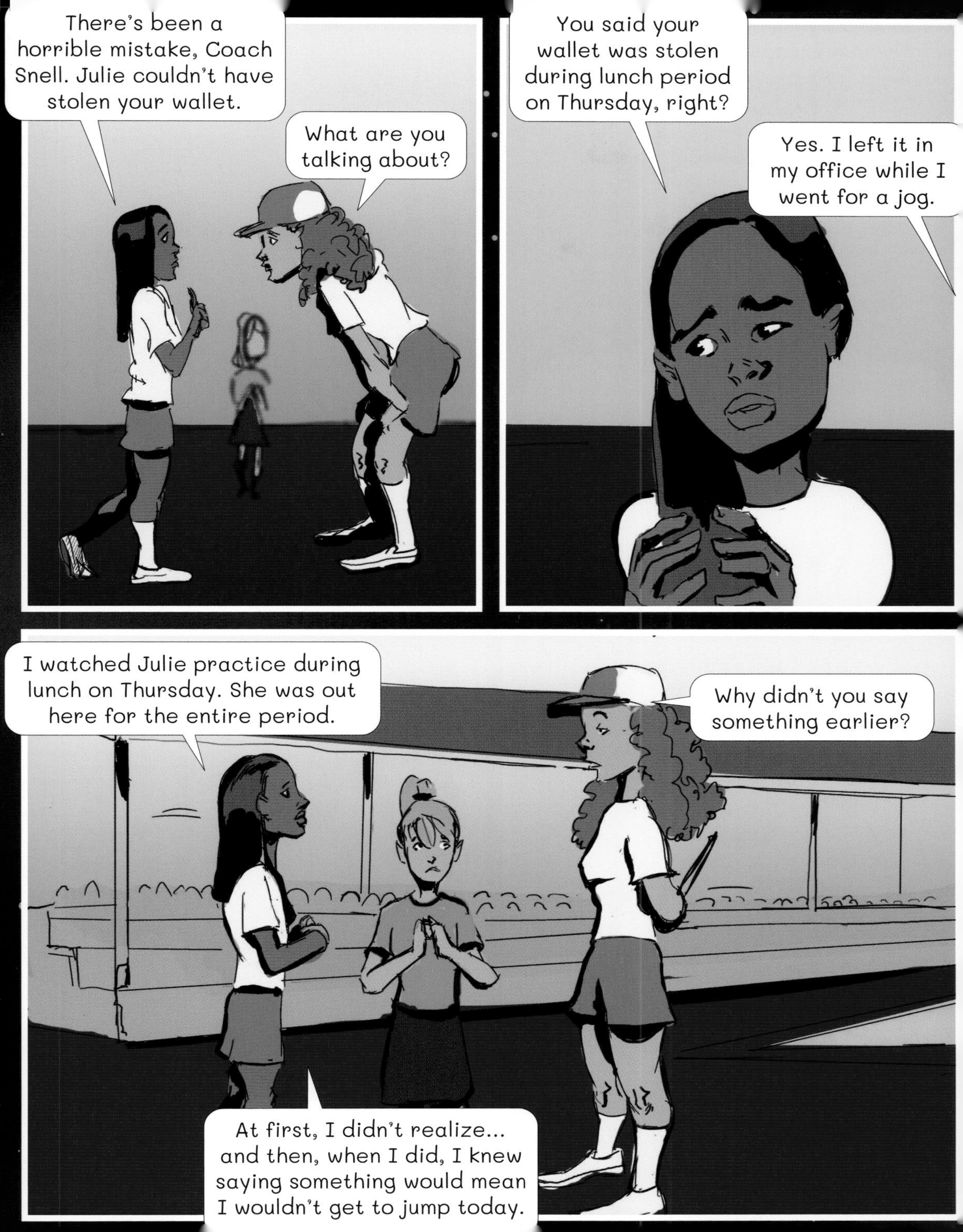
There's been a horrible mistake, Coach Snell. Julie couldn't have stolen your wallet.
What are you talking about?
You said your wallet was stolen during lunch period on Thursday, right?
Yes. I left it in my office while I went for a jog.
I watched Julie practice during lunch on Thursday. She was out here for the entire period.
Why didn't you say something earlier?
At first, I didn't realize... and then, when I did, I knew saying something would mean I wouldn't get to jump today.

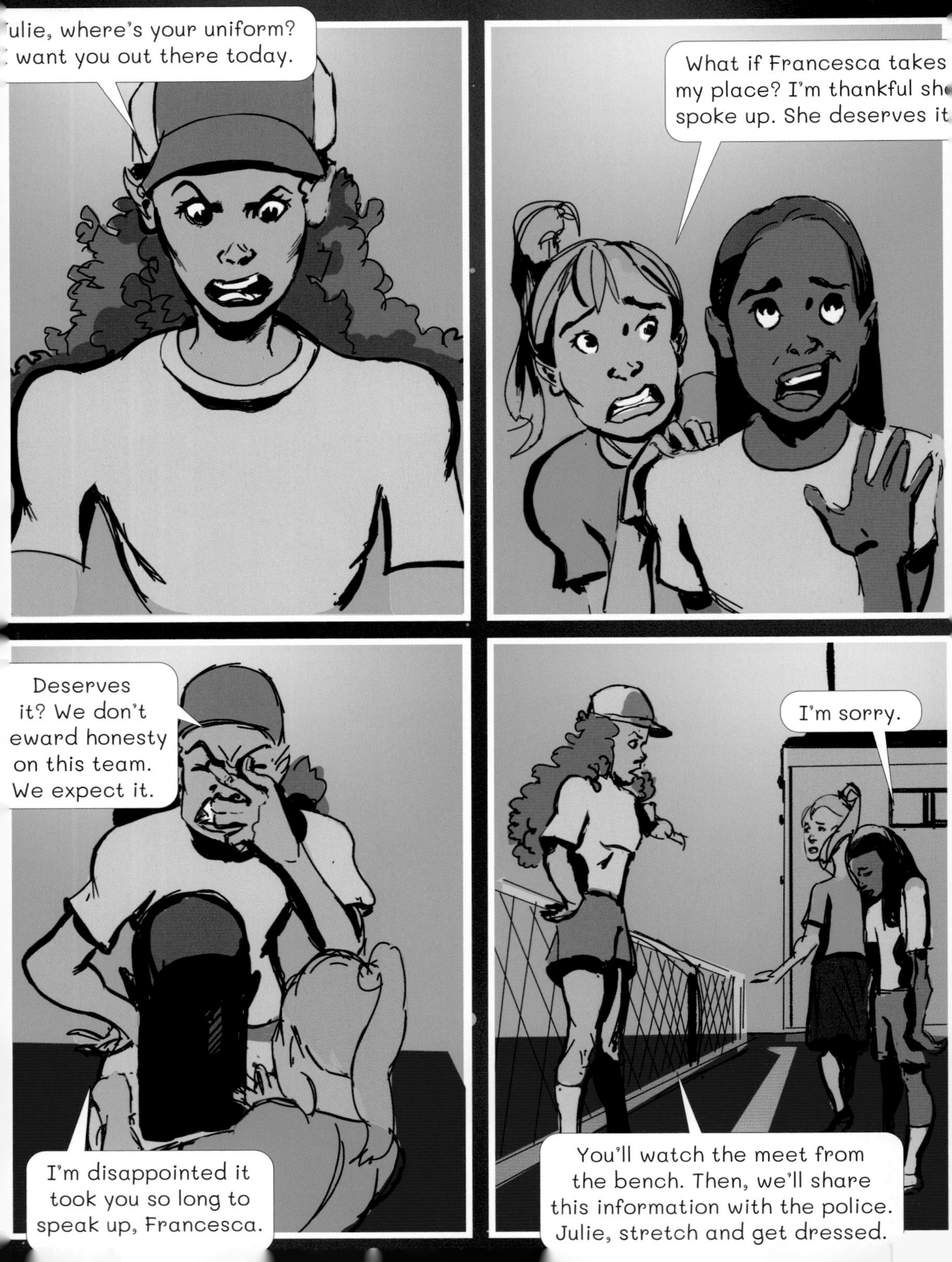
ulie, where's your uniform?
want you out there today.
What if Francesca takes
my place? I'm thankful sh
spoke up. She deserves it
Deserves it? We don't eward honesty on this team. We expect it.
I'm disappointed it took you so long to speak up, Francesca.
I'm sorry.
You'll watch the meet from the bench. Then, we'll share this information with the police. Julie, stretch and get dressed.

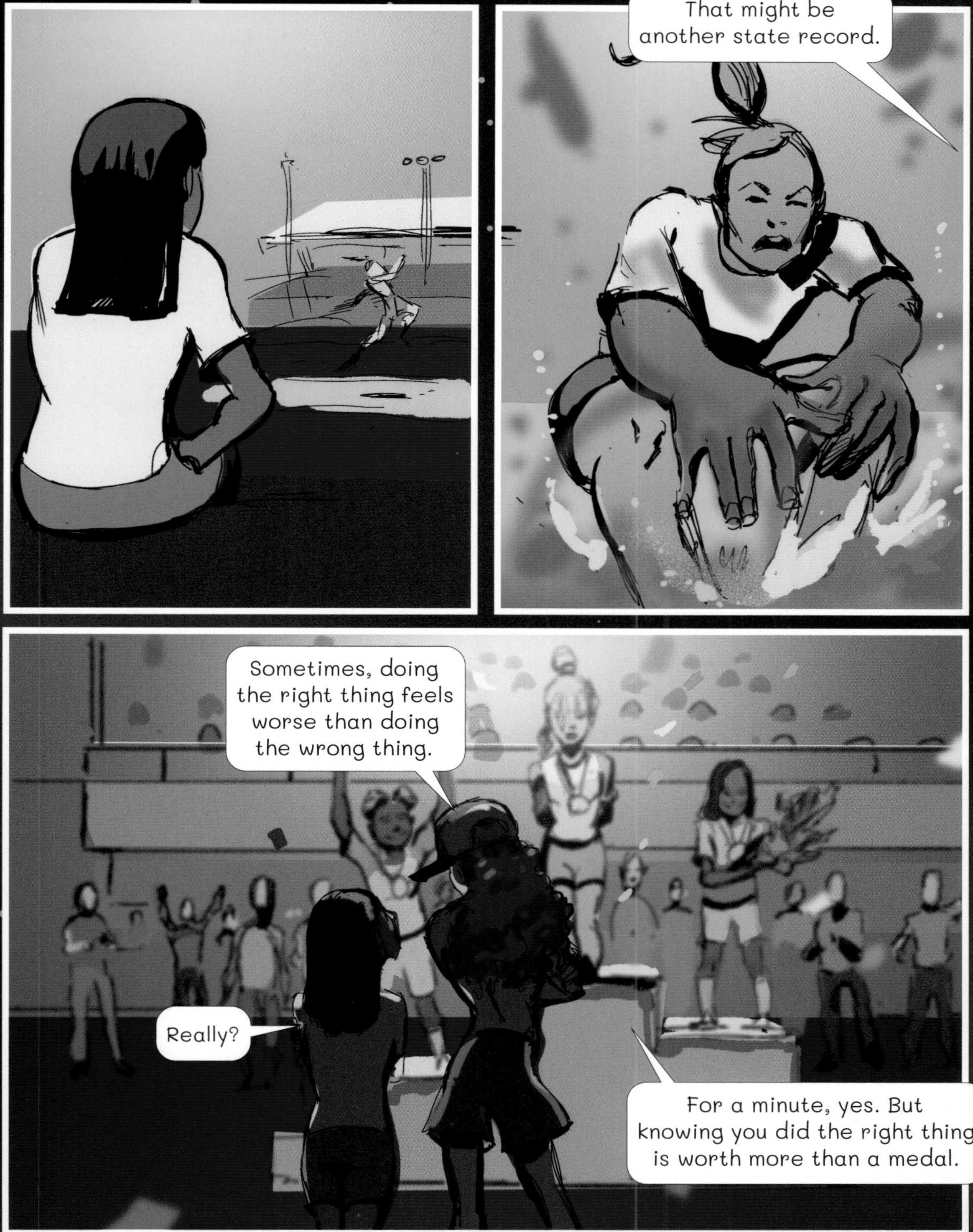
That might be another state record.
Sometimes, doing the right thing feels worse than doing the wrong thing.
Really?
For a minute, yes. But knowing you did the right thing is worth more than a medal.

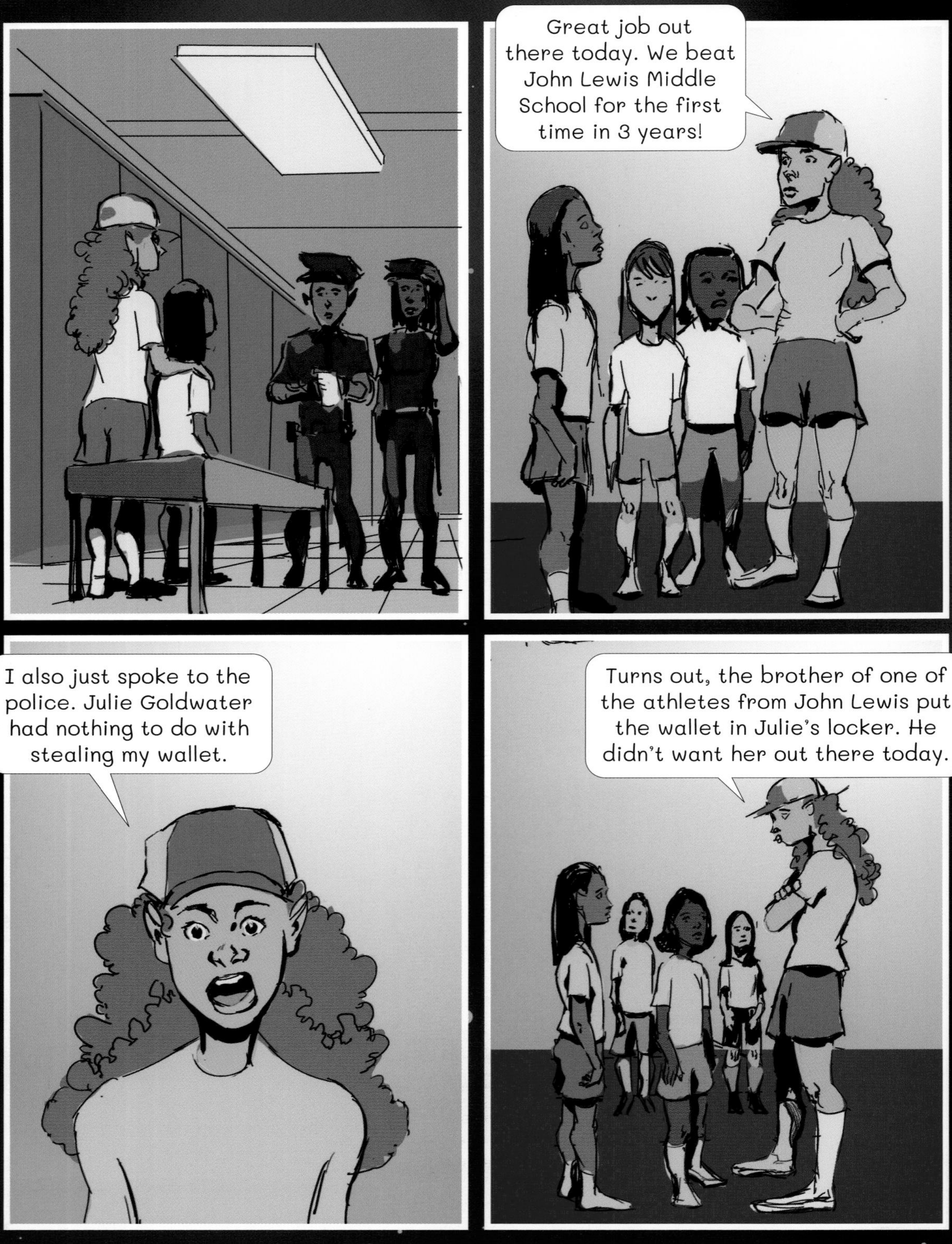
Great job out there today. We beat John Lewis Middle School for the first time in 3 years!
I also just spoke to the police. Julie Goldwater had nothing to do with stealing my wallet.
Turns out, the brother of one of the athletes from John Lewis put the wallet in Julie's locker. He didn't want her out there today.

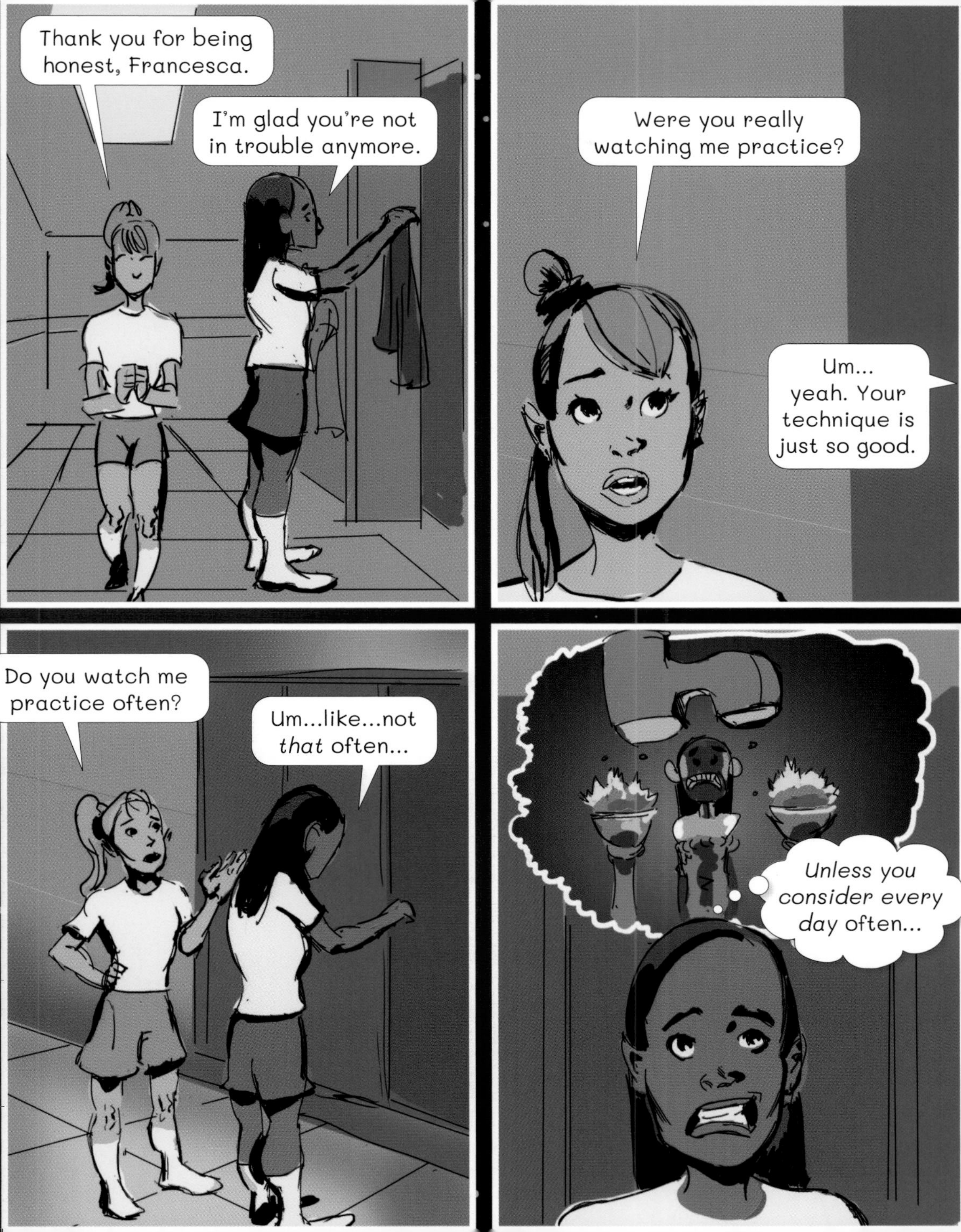
Thank you for being honest, Francesca.
I'm glad you're not in trouble anymore.
Were you really watching me practice?
Um... yeah. Your technique is just so good.
Do you watch me practice often?
Um...like...not *that* often...
Unless you consider every day often...

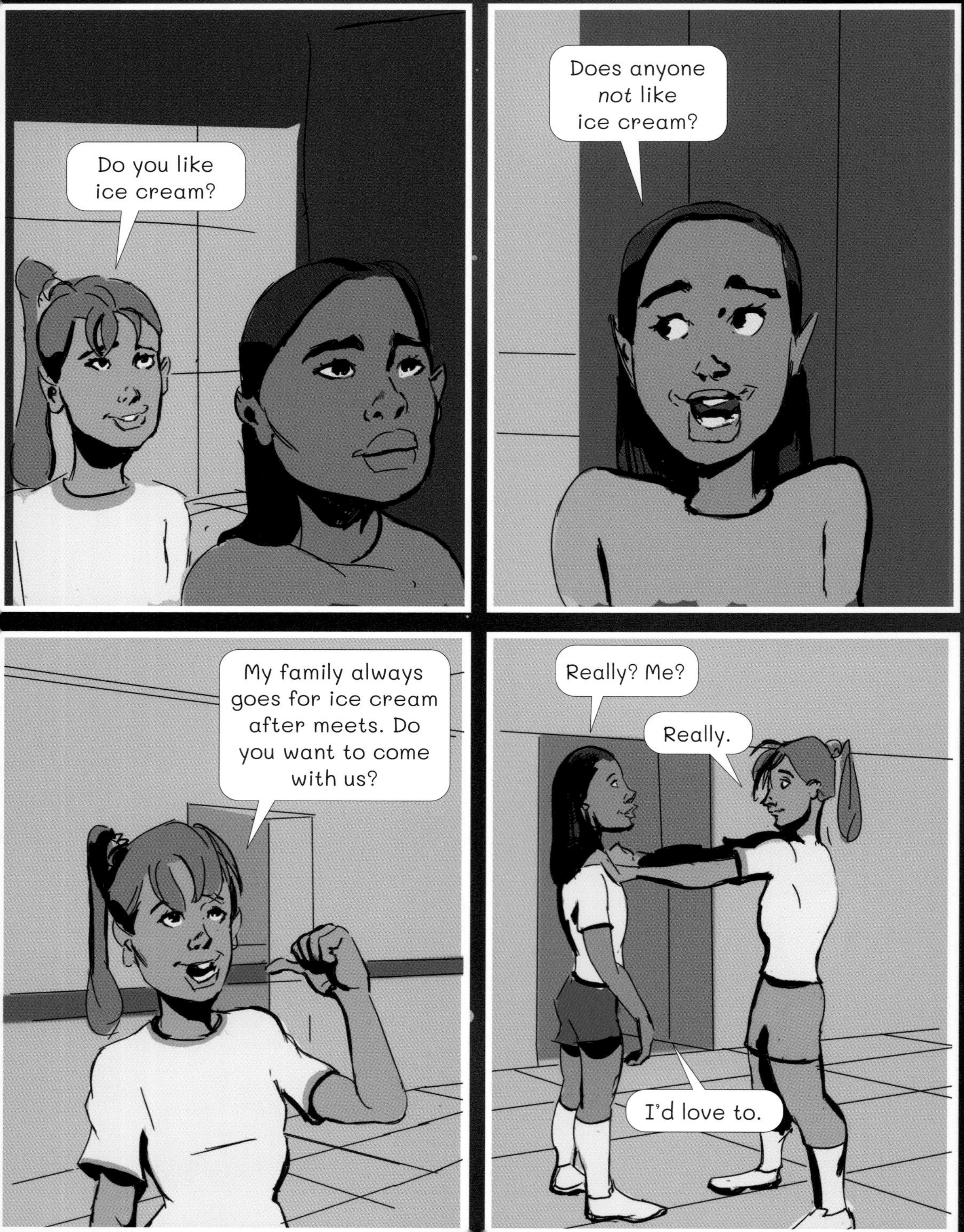
Do you like ice cream?
Does anyone *not* like ice cream?
My family always goes for ice cream after meets. Do you want to come with us?
Really? Me?
Really.
I'd love to.

SPEAK UP

There are many different ways to be honest. One way is by speaking up, even if what you're speaking up about isn't happening to you. Sometimes, a person cannot speak up for themselves. This may be because they are scared. They may think nobody will believe them. They may not know how to describe what happened.

Speaking up can be hard. You may think you're making a big deal out of nothing or getting involved in someone else's business. You may be afraid of getting a person in trouble. But it is always a good idea to tell an adult you trust whenever you see someone who needs your help. This way, the adult can investigate the situation. You may really help someone else just by saying something.

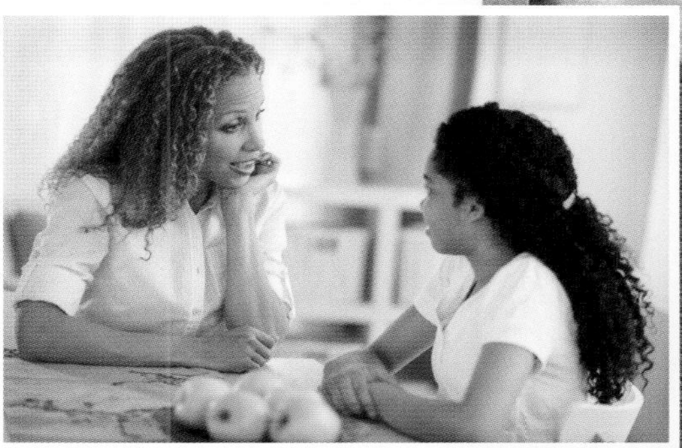

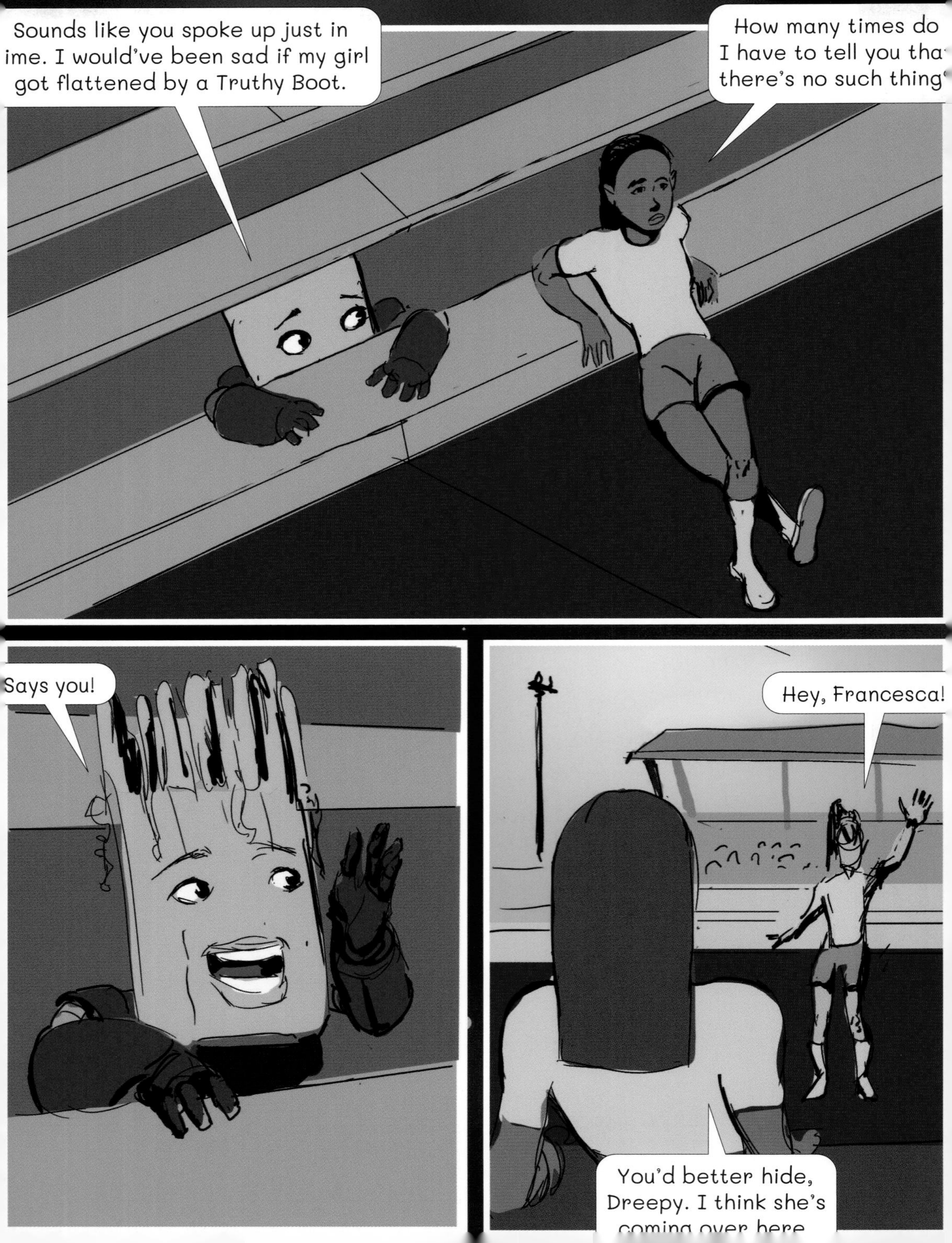
Sounds like you spoke up just in ime. I would've been sad if my girl got flattened by a Truthy Boot.
How many times do I have to tell you tha there's no such thing
Says you!
Hey, Francesca!
You'd better hide, Dreepy. I think she's coming over here

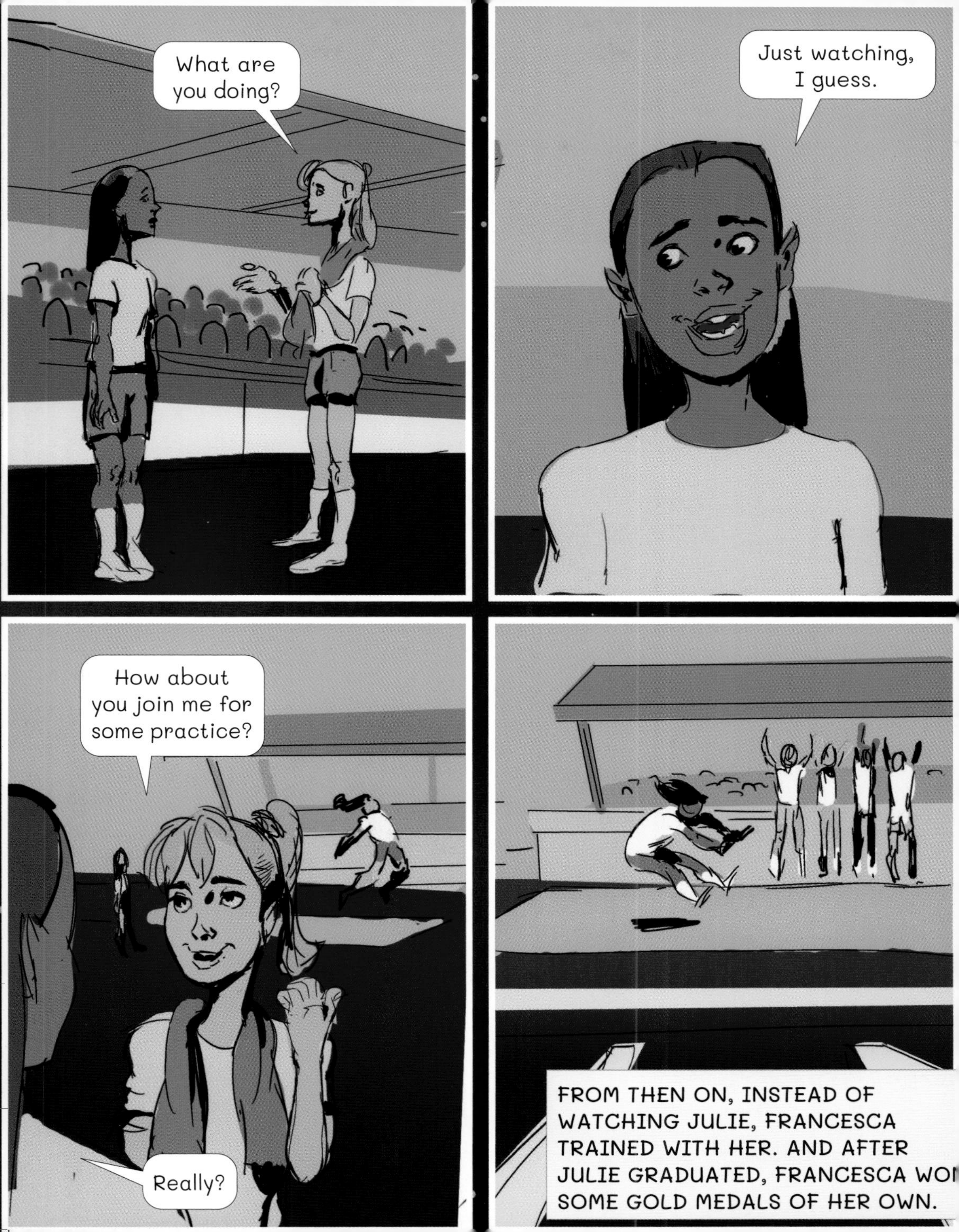
What are you doing?
Just watching, I guess.
How about you join me for some practice?
Really?
FROM THEN ON, INSTEAD OF WATCHING JULIE, FRANCESCA TRAINED WITH HER. AND AFTER JULIE GRADUATED, FRANCESCA WON SOME GOLD MEDALS OF HER OWN.

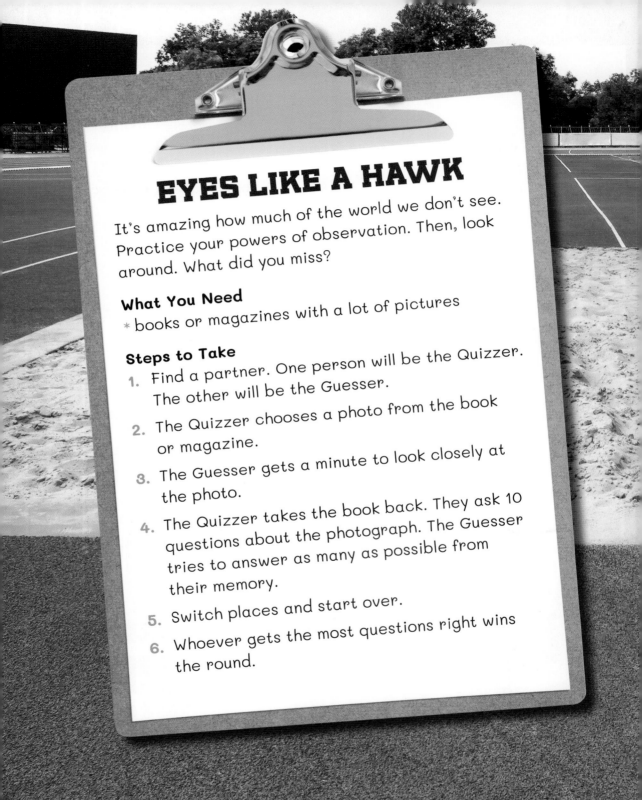

EYES LIKE A HAWK

It's amazing how much of the world we don't see.
Practice your powers of observation. Then, look
around. What did you miss?

What You Need
* books or magazines with a lot of pictures

Steps to Take
1. Find a partner. One person will be the Quizzer. The other will be the Guesser.

2. The Quizzer chooses a photo from the book or magazine.

3. The Guesser gets a minute to look closely at the photo.

4. The Quizzer takes the book back. They ask 10 questions about the photograph. The Guesser tries to answer as many as possible from their memory.

5. Switch places and start over.

6. Whoever gets the most questions right wins the round.

LEARN MORE

BOOKS

Huddleston, Emma. *Legends of Women's Track and Field.* Mendota Heights, MN: Press Box Books, 2021.

Weintraub, Aileen. *We Got Game: 35 Female Athletes Who Changed the World.* Philadelphia, PA: Running Press Kids, 2020.

WEBSITES

Britannica Kids
https://kids.britannica.com/kids/article/track-and-field/353870

Jackie Joyner-Kersee
http://jackiejoynerkersee.com

ALIEN CHARACTERS

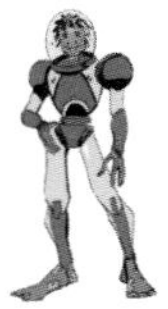

DARNEX
DARNEX IS A HETHITE FROM THE PLANET HETHA. ON HIS HOME PLANET, HE PLAYS THE SPORT WAVE RIDER. HIS BODY MAKES A STICKY GOO THAT SMELLS LIKE PINEAPPLE.

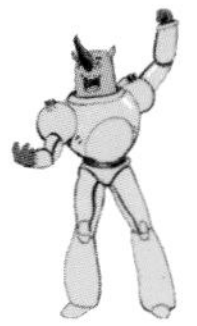

MIKKI
MIKKI IS AN ALIEN FROM PLANET KOPITER. HIS SPORT IS GRILLETTE. HE HAS WORKED HARD TO KEEP HIS COOL UNDER PRESSURE.

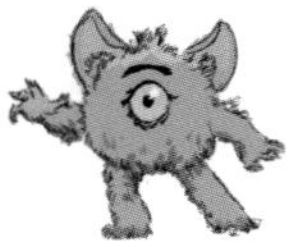

ZANG
ZANG IS AN ALIEN FROM PLANET SMONGTHURP. HE IS A PRO AT THE SPORT FLONGLOG, AND A PRO AT SIGN LANGUAGE.

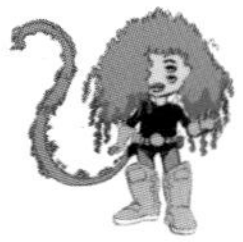

BOLI
BOLI IS AN ALIEN FROM THE PLANET OOH. SHE PLAYS THE TEAM SPORT ZINGER. SHE IS A GREAT TEAMMATE AND FRIEND TO EVERYONE.

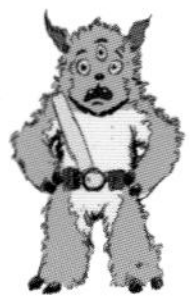

SPLART
SPLART IS AN ALIEN FROM THE PLANET TRASPEN. HE LOVES EATING BACON AND BASEBALLS. HE PLAYS SWAZBUL. IMAGINING FLOWERS AND SANDWICHES HELPS HIM RELAX.

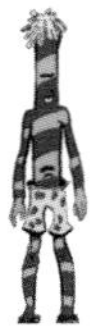

GAMEE GLAP
GAMEE IS AN ALIEN FROM THE PLANET MOOBSTRUM. HE IS A FLARFELL DIVE STAR. HE KNOWS HOW TO HANDLE BULLIES.

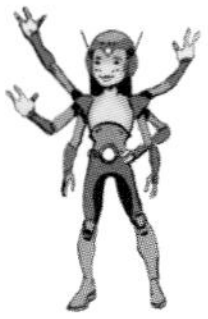

FORBATH
FORBATH IS AN ALIEN FROM THE PLANET EXBERG. SHE PLAYS THE SPORT THREE-SKIFF, WHICH MAKES HER A MASTER MULTITASKER.

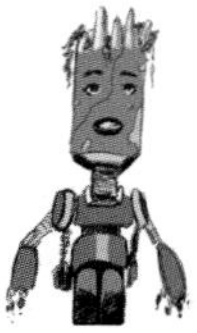

DREEPY
DREEPY IS AN INTERGALACTIC SPORTS STAR, AND SHE KNOWS IT. HER PLANET VALUES HONESTY OVER EVERYTHING. WHO WANTS TO GET SQUASHED BY A TRUTHY BOOT?

GLOSSARY

asthma (AZ-muh) a condition that makes breathing difficult

galaxy (GAL-uk-see) a system of stars and their solar systems

intergalactic (in-tuhr-guh-LAK-tik) between galaxies in space

luster (lust-UHR) shine or soft glow

meteor shower (MEE-tee-uhr SHOW-uhr) a group of space rocks that fall as they enter Earth's atmosphere

momentum (mo-MEHN-tum) the force or speed of motion an object has

plant step (PLANT STEPH) the last step before a jump

suspended (suh-SPEN-dud) not allowed to attend school or be part of a program

INDEX